911
porsche

Osprey Colour Series

911
porsche

clive prew

First published in 1989 by Osprey Publishing Limited
59 Grosvenor Street
London WIX 9DA

British Library Cataloguing in Publication Data

Prew, Clive
   Porsche 911
   1. Porsche 911 cars
   1. Title
   629.2'222

   ISBN 0-85045-924-9

Editor Nicholas Collins
Art Direction Martin Richards
Design Simon Ray-Hills

Printed in Hong Kong

Left
*One of the earliest. 356A after
meticulous restoration.*

Previous page
*RSR Turbo. Only four of these ran in
1974 and they paved the way for the
Group 5 silhouette cars, though we
had to wait until 1976 for the real
thing.*
Martini

First page
*Porsches as far as the eye can see.
Early 356 Speedster heads up a
special display at Fuji, Japan, in
1984.*
Malcolm Bryant

Contents

Introduction & Acknowledgements

For many people there is only one Porsche. For them the 911 is Porsche and everything the name Porsche stands for. The water-cooled cars are only a temporary aberration from which the company will one day recover.

Few cars carry the aura that surrounds the 911. Its history is one of constant development and continual refinement—25 years of making the rear-engined air-cooled idea not only viable but ultimately successful.

Even schoolkids know the 911 story. They can quote the performance figures, how it corners in the wet or the dry, how to slide it round a sharp Alpine hairpin or negotiate the trickier stretches of the 'Ring', not to mention how to tune the ignition or swap the pads. The 911's handling is almost folklore. And tales of bravado at the 911 wheel are as common as they are often exaggerated.

Some say it's the ultimate road car, the epitome of the Teutonic way of doing things. Automotive engineering and design at its best.

Not for Porsche the all-things-to-all-men compromise that has become the 'world car' norm. Nor the fussy, the temperamental or the exotic as characterised by so many Italian sports cars.

If there is one word for it, that word is efficiency. The 911 gets the job done. It's a car for all seasons. Best in the sunshine, but just as content in the wet; perfect for a long haul up the motorway but even better on a curvy country lane. And while it was designed as a road car, its ability on the race track is unquestioned.

Yet for all its competence, the 911 has never quite gained the refinement of its water-cooled brothers. Comfortable—yes, wholly predictable—no. And as many an over-enthusiastic 911 owner has found to his cost, it still demands a certain respect.

But it's more than just speed or handling, it's looks too. The 911 may have been around for over 25 years, but the latest model looks as fresh as the first. Maybe that's the secret. Despite the fact that there is almost no part of the modern 911 that is common with the first, the essence of 911-ness has never been lost. And it's that essence which has turned a mere car into something much more. Something that is going to be with us for a long time yet.

Books of this nature are never just the work of the names on the cover. So words of thanks are due to the many people who helped us in various ways. All of them were only too keen to help, and many of them know a lot more about Porsche cars than we ever will. Thanks then to:

Chris Harvey, Malcolm Bryant, Porsche AG, Porsche Cars Great Britain Ltd, Carreras Rothmans Ltd, Martini and Rossi and assorted others too numerous too mention whose input was indirect but no less important.

Clive Prew and Andrew Moreland.

Left
The only way to do it. Beautifully restored 1964 356 Cabriolet.

Right
A man and his car. Ferdinand Porsche with 1963 Type 901. No wonder he's smiling.

Origins

The Porsche story is one of continuing design evolution and constant model development. No Porsche car demonstrates this philosophy better than the 911. Nowadays it holds a unique reputation as one of the finest, most technologically advanced motor cars of all time, but labels like that are hardly earned overnight.

In some ways the decision to build the 911 was a gamble. Porsche already had one product. The 356, a car that had earned them a good living since 1950 with annual production showing steady growth—298 cars the first year, 7,055 units in 1959 and 9,692 units by 1963. Yet here they were, about to swap the tried and tested for something further up-market, a lot more expensive and powered by a totally new engine.

On the other hand, perhaps it was just commendable foresight—staying well ahead of the game, a policy Porsche have showed a remarkable skill at ever since.

Preliminary styling sketches for what was later to become the 911 are said to date from as early as 1956 (years before the 356B was announced in 1959 and there was still the 356C to come). With 356 body styling that was sure to look dated by the start of the next decade and an old four-cylinder pushrod engine that was fast running out of development room at reasonable cost, Dr Ferry Porsche had not delayed setting out his plans for the new Porsche. After all, by the early 1960s, the competition would have saloons with all the handling and performance of the 356, plus they would be roomier, more comfortable and generally more sophisticated.

Following established Porsche policy, the Type 7 as the new model was designated (Type 6 was the 356C) would be an evolutionary design, that is, it would follow the established Porsche corporate look, but take it a step

Right
Where it all happens. Porsche factory in Stuttgart.

further. Hopefully two steps further.

The wheelbase would not exceed 2.20 metres, yet the car would still qualify as a 'two-plus-two', even though the rear passengers may have to be young children. It would need less maintenance than the 356, incorporate more luggage space, handle better and of course, perform better than any Porsche had ever performed before.

Dr Porsche's eldest son, Ferdinand 'Butzi' Porsche undertook the styling, while the chassis design was left to Reutter Carrosserie. By swapping the old VW-type transverse torsion bar front suspension for a modern design with longitudinal torsion bars acting through the lower wishbones, they managed to increase front luggage space. And by dropping the inherently unstable swing-axle at the rear in favour of an independent set-up with

triangulated semi-trailing arms, they took care of much of the renowned Porsche handling problems. All they required now was something exciting in the engine department. And something exciting is definitely what they got.

In charge of engine development was Ing Hans Tomala. And again, following Dr Porsche's brief, the design was formulated under set parameters. It was to be an air-cooled flat six, much of the design would follow established 356 practice and since it would still be mounted in the rear of the car, it had better be very light in weight too. As for the valve-train, the oiling system, or things like the silencers, they were open to negotiation as the numerous prototypes proved.

By the time the revised Type 7, now named the Porsche 901 was unveiled at the Frankfurt Show in September 1963, the design was set.

Left
Not everyone gets a chance to see what goes on inside the 911 factory. German lineworker wonders how he is ever going to lift that engine and transmission unit into the next 911.

Right
Yet there he is tightening the last few bolts.

Below
Note the extensive paintwork protection in the final building stages.

Above
More body protection. Even the edges of these Turbo arches are defended.

Left
The last few bits of ventilation system are fitted before the headlamp bezels.

Above right
Note how cars are lifted individually and do not travel along a mechanised line.

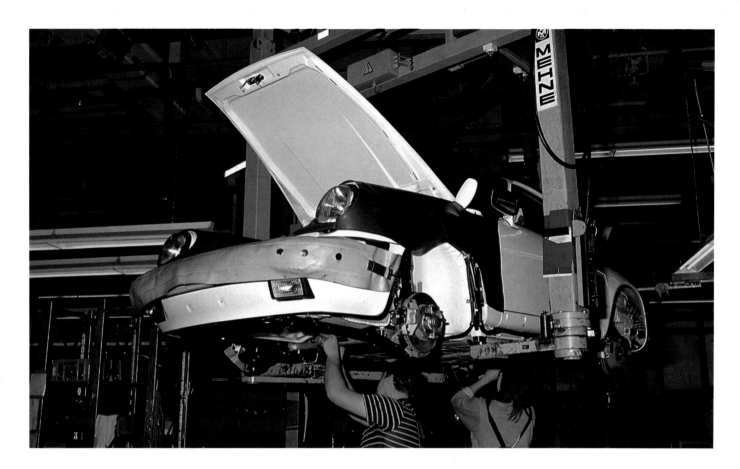

Butzi's slightly ungainly prototype had been re-styled into the beautiful shape we now know as the 911 and Ferdinand Piech (Dr Porsche's nephew) had refined the engine into the first production 2-litre Porsche flat six.

Even though it was not to be available for sale for at least another 12 months, the car was already being marked a success. True to form, it retained a Porsche family likeness. They could have named it the 356D as it retained that some high front wing line, the deeply sloping bonnet and the smooth gradual curve from roof to rear bumper. The bumpers were almost fared-in versions of the 356C examples, in the same way that the flush-fitting front grilles and indicators were the next logical step from the jutting previous ones. Even the rear side windows reminded you of the 356, retaining that same curve at the rear corner.

Yet as much as it harked back to previous models, the 901 was very much styled for the future. It had 50 per cent more glass area and generally sharper lines all around. It was 2.4 inches narrower than the 356, the wheels seemed to fit the arches better and the rear lid extended right down to bumper level for improved engine access. Certainly, the design was to be improved, honed and generally updated for many years to come, but the basis was there from the start for what is undoubtedly one of the most purposeful looking sports cars the world has seen.

In the engineering department, the story was the same. Four-wheel disc brakes, ZF rack and pinion steering with a double-jointed column and new front suspension design with lower wishbones, McPherson strut-type damper location and an anti-roll bar were all part of

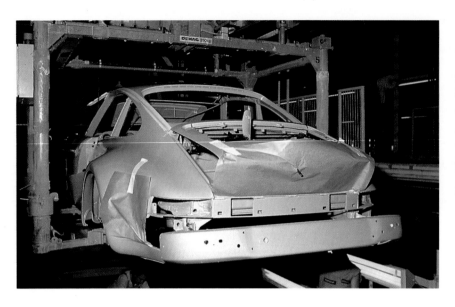

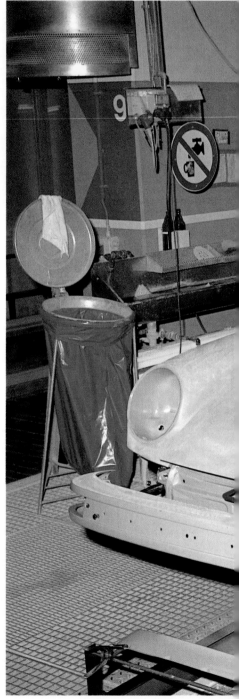

Above
After the primer, bodyshell gets a bit of extra paintwork.

Right
Flatting the primer before the final colour coats are added.

Below
They do not just paint the top either.

Above
In the aftermarket these cylinder heads complete with cam housings are worth more than some complete new cars.

Left
Assembled and balance cranks await installation.

the new design, along with fully independent rear suspension, a new five-speed gearbox and a Fichtel and Sachs single dry-plate clutch. Wheels were skinny $4\frac{1}{2} \times$ 15 inch steels; tyres were 165 HR 15s.

Then there was the engine: 1991 cc through a bore and stroke of 80 × 66 mm, a vertically-split cast aluminium crank case and a forged steel crank with eight bearings. The compression ratio was set at 9:1, and the six pistons ran in individual 'Biral' cylinders—finned aluminium with cast iron liners. The first

Above
Take your pick. Cylinder head waiting for cam housings.

Right
More cylinder heads. Note the hemispherical chambers.

engines had two Solex PI 40 mm overflow-type carburettors (not the most successful set-up Porsche ever developed) with two mechanical fuel pumps driven by the left-hand camshaft.

Power output may have been lowly by modern day Porsche standards, but for 1963 it certainly gave the competition something to think about. Not only that but at 130 bhp (6100 rpm) and 128 lb ft of torque (4200 rpm), the design had left plenty of room for improvement. In fact, in later years Dr Porsche is quoted as saying that had he known the lengths to which development of that same basic design would go, those first engines would

have been less sturdy in construction.

Finally available in the autumn of 1964, 901 had become 911. Peugeot had copyrighted all combinations of three numbers with a 0 in the middle, hence the change of designation. But it did not matter one bit. The press loved it and so did the public. Though to hedge bets Porsche also offered the 912, a 911 with a slightly detuned 356C engine.

The new 911 was fast—some said as quick as the old Carrera—yet it retained a business-like reliability with none of the fuss and temperament of its peers. It had modern good looks yet in no way was it extreme or impractical. And above all, it was a true sports car. Built to be driven. And driven hard.

If there were gripes they were usually limited to the respect-provoking handling and an unfortunate carburation flat spot caused by the Solex carburettors. Despite the changes in suspension design, many 911 owners learned that lifting off mid-corner meant exiting backwards travel. Though with that combination of narrow tyres, short wheelbase and rear engine they could hardly have expected anything different. You did not need to drive enthusiastically to discover the joys of 911 understeer either. Porsche did effect a part cure for this for customers who complained with sufficient vehemence, but flush-fitting an 11 kg weight to each end of the front bumper was hardly the long term answer.

Left
*Transaxle complete with rear cradle
and starter motor.*

Right
*Attention to heads before the cam
housings are bolted on.*

Left
Sophisticated engine shop makes full use of energy saving machinery.

Above
Crank is in, the case is bolted together and the pistons are next.

Right
Barrels are on, next is head and cam housing assembly.

Whatever the grievancies, they certainly did not effect demand. In fact, Porsche had so many orders in the first year that they were unable to cope, despite taking over the Reutter body factory, which effectively doubled their production capacity. To ensure adequate supplies of bodyshells, they eventually had to contract Karmann to produce them independently with final assembly taking place at Zuffenhausen near Stuttgart.

Left
Second cam housing gets the treatment.

Above
Making it look very easy. Note all the distributors ready for installation.

So, if it was ever a gamble, it was certainly
one that paid off. Production for 1966, the first
full year of 911 and 912 production, totalled
13,134 cars. The 911 had arrived. And Porsche
had embarked on a journey that would take the
company through over twenty-five years of
continuous testing, revision, adjustment and of
course, improvement.

Emergence

With the subsequent rise of the 911, it is easy to pass over its humbler brother the 912. Yet in 1965 it was just as important a part of the Porsche line-up. Volumes sold that first year actually beat 911 sales by a sizeable margin, with even better figures to follow as the car was type approved for the USA. In 1966 Porsche built just over 13,000 cars, of which more than 9,000 had only four cylinders.

Part of its attraction must have been the price. For only DM 16,250 you could swan about in what to all intents and purposes looked exactly like DM 22,900 worth of new 911. Using a detuned version of the old four-cylinder 356 SC engine, the 912 managed nearly 120 mph with a 0–60 mph of around 12 seconds. Not as fast as the 911, of course, but it was two cylinders and about 40 horsepower light. In all other respects, the 912 was the same. Same brakes, same suspension, same steering and presumably the same handling peculiarities. The interior was slightly less exotic than the 911, but at over DM 6,500 cheaper, you could hardly complain.

In some ways it was a pity that the 912 was so shortlived. By the time it was discontinued in 1968 to make way for the new VW/Porsche 914 and 916 models, 912 production had reached 30,300 in both Coupe and Targa versions so it obviously had its admirers, not to mention a valued place in the growing Porsche range.

What is also interesting is that in a move almost unique in automotive history, Porsche reintroduced the 912 some six years later, once the 914 had been finally put to rest. Introduced for the US market only as a stop-gap until the new 924 was available, the new 912 E still only had four-pot power, but this time in the form of the 90 bhp 2-litre VW Type 4 engine. The same unit that had powered the 914. As only 2,099 cars were produced before the 1976 launch

Left
Spot the difference. The first Carreras. Lightweight RS at the front with Touring version at the back.
Chris Harvey

of the 924, you cannot help wondering if it was worth the effort.

The 911, meanwhile, had gone from strength to strength. Hardly was the 911 Coupe on sale when Porsche introduced a new model, the 911 Targa. Announced at the 1965 Frankfurt Show, the Targa was designed by Butzi Porsche as a replacement for the 356C Cabriolet. It was not a true cabriolet, of course, as it retained the wide rollbar with its smart brushed stainless steel finish. But the roof did lift out in two separate halves, and the rear window was made of flexible plastic and could be unzipped.

Porsche emphasised this point with its 'four personalities' marketing spiel. There was the Targa Spyder, a fully open car with the roof off and the rear window folded flat; the Targa Bel Air with the top off but the rear window in place to eliminate the buffeting common to all convertibles where the wind rushes back at you from the rear of the car; the Targa Voyage, with top on but rear window down, and the Targa Hardtop with both top and window firmly in place. Four cars for the price of one.

Right
Two years' worth of Carrera RS—2.7 and 3.0-litre.

Below
In fine detail. Carrera RS alloy five-spoke wheel.

Right
*Porsche 914/6. Body by VW, engine
by Porsche. In this case, a special
190 bhp, 2.4-litre version, replacing
the correct 2.0-litre 911T.*

Below
*Same car, different view. There are
probably only 10 of these cars in the
UK, while the USA, Germany and
France share the rest between them.*

No wonder it was so popular, making up nearly 40 per cent of 911 sales by 1967.

The next new model came in 1967. Porsche had always based the range on a three-tier line-up. Previously it was 356 Normal, Super and Super 90. So as we already had the 911 and the 912, it was only natural that sooner or later we would see a hotter 911 to complete the range.

The 911 S was that and more—30 horsepower more at a total of 160 bhp thanks to higher compression, new camshafts with more overlap and new Weber IDA 30 3C carbs. Introduced as standard fitment on all 911s, they finally rid it of those dreadful Solex flat-spots. On the outside, the new 911 S forged alloy five-spoke wheels allowed more air around the vented front discs, while underneath, it benefitted from a front anti-roll bar and Koni dampers.

A top speed of 140 mph, 0–60 mph in eight seconds and the quarter mile in under 16 seconds were more than enough to earn the 911 S a solid reputation for sporting performance. Though its penchant for fouling plugs with alarming regularity earned it a reputation of a different kind.

Other news for 1967 was that August saw the launch of what Porsche called the A-series cars. Previous 911s were O-series. The A-series line-up included the 911 S, of course, but introduced two new models. One was the 911 L (for Luxus or Luxury), a basic 911 with upmarket S-type trim, the other was the 911 T (for Touring). In a way the 911 T was the six cylinder 912. It had the same cheaper interior, solid disc brakes and only the four-speed gearbox, but a low-cost version of the 911 L engine with only 110 bhp. On the other hand, it was cheap, the first 911 below DM 20,000.

As far as vehicle specification went, 1967 was also the first year for $5\frac{1}{2}$J wheels, various exterior trim revisions and a new semi-automatic gearbox.

The 'Sportomatic' combined the best of both worlds. A four-speed manual gearbox with a

Left
Photographer's own 911 RS lurks in the grass near Stuttgart. Chris Harvey

torque converter and no clutch pedal. This Type 905 transmission used a microswitch and servo mechanism to disengage the clutch the moment you grabbed the gear lever. Performance was only marginally effected, once you learned the technique of actually using the thing, and once Porsche had proved its reliability, it became quite popular with some drivers. Though unfortunately not popular enough to save it from being discontinued in 1979.

In 1968 it was all change once again. The new B-series cars incorporated a whole list of new improved features. It was fast becoming obvious that Porsche were not prepared to just design the car and let it stay that way for long. These new cars had a longer wheelbase, slightly flared arches, a new magnesium crankcase, a revised steering rack and better brakes, weight distribution and handling. The Targas gained a new solid wraparound rear windscreen this year and there was even a totally new model, the 911 E.

Keeping track of all the 911 model designations was never the simplest of tasks, especially as the US market received different cars at different times with different spec thanks to the effects of emmissions control. They also quote model years from the date new models were announced, usually part way through the year before.

Replacing the 911 L, 911 E stood for *Einspritzung* or injection (a new Bosch mechanical system) which upped the power of this model from 130 to 140 bhp. The 911 S now boasted 170 bhp, while the third model in the new line-up, the 911 T, remained the same with carburettors and a measly 110 bhp.

The 911 E also announced a new departure in the suspension department. Self-levelling hydro-pneumatic front struts provided a softer ride

Right
Impex 911 Cabriolet. The full package for people with full wallets.

Inset
Thinking about it . . . make that 'very fat wallets'.

for the 911 E driver, as part of the Comfort Package, standard on all 911 Es and optional on others. Along with the struts, which used the up and down movement of the suspension to keep the pump pressurised, 911 E drivers got 14 inch wheels, ventilated discs with aluminium calipers and a whole array of minor comfort and convenience items like leather-covered steering wheel and extra gauges. But despite their ingenius design the new struts never really found favour with Porsche enthusiasts and were dropped in 1971.

So, acceleration was brisker, handling was obviously improved thanks to the better weight distribution and the engine was actually running better thanks to assorted changes in that department. Yet would Porsche wait for the competition to catch up? Certainly not. In September 1969, it was all change once again.

In what would be the first of many increases in engine capacity, the 911 was increased to 2195 cc, mainly to give the US emissions engine a bit more go. The European cars benefited to even greater effect, of course. The 911 T, now with twin Zenith carbs went up to 125 bhp, the 911 E went up to 155 and the 911 S to no less than 180 bhp. There were also modifications to the suspension where the upper strut mount was moved forward for better steering response.

Perhaps of greater significance, as any early Porsche owners would confirm, was that 1969 was the first year of some sort of anti-rust treatment. Not the kind of full galvanising seen later but significant nevertheless.

Upping the capacity to combat the effects of ever stricter US emissions regulations was to become almost commonplace during the 1970s. In 1971, an increased stroke gave the 911 2341 cc, or 2.4-litres as it was somewhat optimistically called. By 1973 a new Porsche had 2.7-litres and by 1975 if you were lucky enough to order the re-introduced Carrera, it came with 3-litres. The 930 turbo cars eventually grew to 3.3 litres, of course, but that was later.

Left
DP Motorsport Cabriolet.

Above

The unmistakable 911 Turbo. Launched at the Paris Show in October 1974, it was only meant as a homologation special for the early turbo racers, but has outlived them by years. Motor

More cubic inches was not the only change. Going back to 1971, the 2.4-litre cars had reduced compression ratios enabling them to run on 2-star petrol and an alteration was made in the location of the oil tank and filler. Unfortunately it now looked too much like a petrol filler, with obvious results, so they moved it back to the rear of the right-hand wing the following year. Boge dampers were now fitted as standard, and the 911 S made history as the first production car in the world to feature a front spoiler, albeit barely more than a lip on the bottom of the front valance. It worked, as tests proved, and it was no time at all before every car in the 911 range featured spoilers of some kind.

Relocation of the oil tank was reversed in 1972, and was almost the only modification as far as the 'normal' 911s went. A stainless exhaust system was fitted that year along with a new 80-litre fuel tank and new black horn grilles, but it was not revisions to the existing models that set tongues wagging that year, there was something a lot more exciting to talk about.

1972 was Carerra year with three hot new models aimed at cleaning up in European

Championship GT racing. Based on the 911 S the Carrera RS boasted 2.7-litres and 210 bhp, while its even more serious brother, the Carerra RSR developed over 300 bhp.

By 1973, it was not just the Carrera that could boast 2.7-litres. The new G-Series cars were perhaps the most radically different new models since the 911 began. For a start the range was rationalised. Out was the 911 T and the 911 E and in came the basic 911 to join the S and Carrera, which for the 1974 model year had lost its RS designation but gained a few comforts.

Also deleted from the build inventory was the old mechanical fuel injection, making way for the latest Bosch K-Jetronic system which

Above

You will not see too many of these down at the local pub. An 1989 spec 911 Speedster with laid back screen and hump back.

thanks to its improved fuel metering kept the 911 the right side of the US emissions regulations.

From the outside, the 1973/74 cars are simple to distinguish from their predecessors as yet another concession to US regulations brought in the enlarged aluminium crash protection bumpers, which in the UK at least were shock absorbing so they could spring back in the event of a light impact. Those famous front grilles, a Porsche trade mark since the very earliest days, were another victim of the 1973 restyle.

911 Cabriolet. Porsche's return to
proper fresh air motoring took some
18 years.
Motor

On the other hand, what went on to the new cars was a lot more significant than what came off. A front air dam, a larger two-gallon washer reservoir, high bucket seats, a single 12-volt battery instead of the two as before, inertia reel seat belts, different facia knobs and switches were all part of the 1974 spec.

Although the new 911 model had taken over from the old 911 E in terms of specification, none of the new cars were particularly faster for all their new capacity. Fuel economy, tractability and general 'driveability' were all better, but power output certainly was not. Both 911 and 911 S actually came with less horsepower than their 2.4-litre equivalents—911 at 150 bhp and 911 S at 175 bhp. And the US spec cars were even worse, though it has to be said that at least the Carrera kept the side up with a reasonably healthy 210 bhp.

210 bhp probably appeared quite decent as far as road-going 911s were concerned until 1974. But the new 930, or 911 Turbo as it became better known, changed everyone's expectations at a stroke. Introduced at the Paris Motor Show in October 1973 the new 3-litre 930 was just about all they had to talk about that year as the 911 got a new heater, a bigger alternator and very little else.

After the constant excitment of the first decade, the following ten years of 911 development were limp in comparison. The fact of it was that by now the 911 was getting ever nearer to that ideal of the perfect sports car. Modifications became more subtle, changes did not happen in large steps, but slight increments. More in the way of minor tuning, or to use the Porsche phrase, 'optimising', than major redesign work.

In 1975 the 911 S was finally dropped, though the new 165 bhp 911 did a pretty fair impersonation of it. The Turbo was the top of the range, of course, leaving a gap for a middle model, the new 3-litre Carrera 3. Modifications generally were restricted to an uprated oil

pump and slight adjustments to the fuel injection, brakes and front suspension, but as was said, it was fine-tuning rather than hefty redesign. The best thing about the 1976 model year cars is that they were the first to be constructed totally of Thyssen double-side hot galvanised steel. And to prove it did the job, they even left a bare unpainted shell outside at the Weissach testing facility to prove how long it would last. The fully painted production versions were offered with a comprehensive six year anti-corrosion warranty.

With 1976 revisions limited to new anti-theft door mechanisms, refinement of gearbox parts and a brake servo for left-hand drive Sportomatic-equipped cars, it is to 1977 that we must look for the next significant developments. For the 1978 model year, the Carerra designation was dropped once again. So was the old 2.7-litre 911. In its place came a single normally-aspirated model, the 911 SC, while the Turbo went up to 3.3-litres.

The 911 SC was a Carrera in everything but name. Slightly detuned at 180 bhp, but just the same mechanically even down to the wide wheels and electric windows. In fact with its higher, flatter torque curve the loss in power went virtually unnoticed. As expected, the servo became standard that year too, thankfully not overpowering the brakes but helping when they were cold.

The lack of development throughout the late 1970s is indicative of Porsche's plans for the car at that time. With the 924 selling well at the lower end of the market, and the 928 growing steadily at the top, the 911 was caught between the two. And as the 944 was set for an early 1980s debut with its Turbo counterpart to follow in 1985, the 911 would be steadily run down. It was only in 1980, when Dr Ferry Porsche dictated that the 911 would stay that development took off once again.

At a stroke, 911 SC horsepower went from 188 to 204 bhp for the 1981 model year.

Above
A sunny day, a 911, the open road and the number plate on everyone's Christmas list.
Motor

Left
Preferred by many enthusiasts, the pre-1974 911 has a design cleanliness that the later cars never quite matched.
Autocar

Below
A 1988 Cabriolet Turbo. It took nearly two decades before Porsche finally admitted that the Cabriolet body was up to turbo power
Motor

Maximum speed went up to 146 mph yet fuel consumption was improved too. And soon after there was a whole new variant family added to the model line-up.

The first proper Porsche convertible for nearly 18 years, the 911 SC Cabriolet began life as a prototype at the 1981 Frankfurt Show, featuring not only the hand-operated convertible top but also four-wheel drive. Only six months later the car was announced at the 1982 Geneva Show. It had lost its four-wheel drive but none of its appeal as sales figures proved. In the first full year of production, 4,277 Cabriolets were sold and only 2,752 Targas. Strangely enough, the following year showed more Targas than Cabriolets sales, but it made no odds. The Cabriolet was here to stay.

911 Cabriolet. There must be worse ways to spend your money.

Basically, today's design is just as interesting in all other areas as its predecessors. The 1989 911 Carrera has Bosch L-Jetronic fuel injection, electronically optimised by the Digital Motor Electronics (DME) computer, the disc brakes are thicker with a system to help reduce front wheel lockup in the wet, and in the body department you can order Turbo arches to match optional Turbo suspension. The 911 even comes with early 928-type 'telephone dial' wheels now as standard.

As if to prove to the world that the 911 was

Wild Targa customising from BB of Germany
Chris Harvey

set for a very long life, the Carrera set out to put the 911 right at the top of the performance motoring tree. For a start, the capacity was increased for the fifth time in the car's history to 3164 cc, or following Porsche's typically optimistic valuations, 3.2-litres. Naturally the power was up, this time to 231 bhp, torque rose to 209 lb ft at 4800 rpm and yet once again, all this was achieved with savings in fuel consumption, taking the new 911 back to 1965 in terms of miles per gallon.

The 1989 model year Porsche 911 catalogue says everything there is to say about one of the world's best loved cars. There may be bigger and better models now, with Speedsters, Cabriolets, even flat-nosed Cabriolets with Super Sport Equipment joining the traditional Coupes and Targas in the 911 line-up. There may be 231 bhp where once there was only 130. And there may be electric switches where there used to be window winders. But as even the most cursory glance will prove, the 911 is really the same as it has always been. That same six cylinder engine with dry sump lubrication. That same body shell with raised wings over a sloping bonnet, funny rear side windows and front quarterlights. And most of all that same 911 spirit. The spirit that for most people epitomises what Porsche motoring is all about.

Above
Just after the first major restyle. A 2.7-litre coupe with fat US-style bumpers and ATS pressure cast cookie-cutter wheels (standard fitment from 1974).

Right
PEP. The Porsche Experimental Prototype consists of four modules. The drive and chassis, the central body, the rear axle and the front axle. All fuel and brake line connections are the quick-release, aircraft-type so modules can be swapped. Even the throttle is worked electronically.

PEP's basic driveline module is laid out for four-wheel drive, while the engine sits on top of the gearbox piggy back style. More than that, the transaxle tube and shift rods telescope so Porsche can adjust the wheelbase from 2537 mm right down to 2297 mm, or shorter if you only want two-wheel drive.

Following page inset
There is obviously little in the way of interior comfort, except for the 912 steering column and instruments.

Following page
PEP can test numerous aspects of car design from four-wheel drive torque split to different weight distributions. Body rigidity can be compared under different roll conditions and the external skin can be altered to test lift and aerodynamics on the road.

Competition

Both Carrera and Turbo exist because of motor sport. With European Championship GT racing playing such a large part in building the 911 image, Porsche naturally needed ever quicker models with which to compete. And racing cars need swift road cars to homologate them.

The Carrera was the car that was meant to give the keynote to the racing programme but not everything went to plan. There had been Porsche Carreras almost as long as there had been Porsches. 1955 saw the launch, though the concept went right back to 1952. The 911 version did not arrive until 1972, though needless to say, it was well worth the wait.

The original plan was to build 500 stripped-out racing-type 911 S's with bigger engines, better handling and more power as a homologation exercise for European Group 4 GT racing. In the end, nearly 1,600 Carrera RSs were built on their own production line, of which 1,036 were the magical M471 RS Sport or 'lightweight' versions. Of these 49 were then converted to the even more magical 2.8-litre M491 RS Rennsport versions, while the rest, the M472 Touring versions, were more like the 911 S in terms of comfort.

To say that the Carrera RS was well received would be more than understatement. For a start, it came with the potency of 2687 cc. The stroke remained the same as the production 911 S at 70.4 mm, but Porsche devised a way of increasing the bore an extra 6 mm to 90 mm by doing away with the Biral cylinder liners and coating the bare aluminium walls with nickel-silicone carbide or Nikasil as it was known. The result not only gained the extra space to increase the bore but also reduced friction and wear in the cylinder. The rest of the engine was much the same as the contemporary 911 S design but the increased capacity resulted in another 20 bhp and brought the total to 210.

Le Mans in 1986. The ultimate expression of the 959 concept, the racing 961.
Malcolm Bryant

With the lightweight version reduced to only 900 kg, it was hardly surprising that the Carrera RS turned in some pretty impressive performance figures—0–60 mph took only 6 seconds, and you did not fully run out of steam till you had reached 150 mph. Speed like that did not go without compromises in the luxury department, of course, but then luxury was not what Carrera was about. To make that 900 kg weight break there was no sound deadening whatsoever, nor anything like door trim, glove-box lid or even a rear seat. The front seats were skinny affairs that held you in but did not offer much in the way of padding, the sheet metal and windscreen were thinner and the engine cover was fibreglass and incorporated a distinctive 'ducktail' spoiler.

Handling was of obvious importance as the car was destined for the track and the rear spoiler gave it more than just sporty looks. Tests proved that it reduced lift at the rear of the car by some 70 per cent at top speed with added benefits in high speed stability, especially in cross-winds. With wider rear 7 inch wheels, heavier anti-roll bars at 18 mm and Bilstein dampers, cornering was improved dramatically.

For a car that began with such an exciting and impressive specification at its launch, it must have saddened many a Porsche enthusiast that only one year later, the emasculation had begun. Apart from new bumpers and styling common to all new G-series cars, the 1974 model year Carrera was given all the usual 911 trimmings and comforts. The power output was the same and Porsche even gave it a heavier front anti-roll bar, but the lightweight spirit went that year along with the RS designation. The new Carrera even had electric windows.

To be fair, there was a Carrera RS for 1974 but as only 44 of the road-going versions were

Right
No point having go without show, and the DP Motorsport Targa has more than its fair share of both. 935 type nose, Turbo arches and sill extensions are only the start.

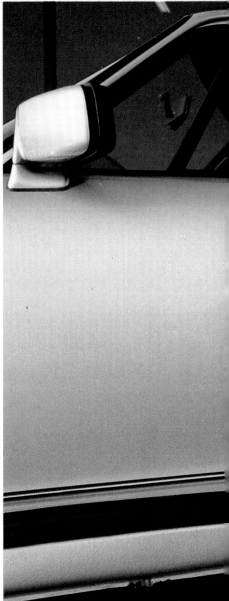

Above
The 1987 911 Turbo SE. Well over a hundred grand and counting.

Left
911 Turbo SE finally gave Porsche a new nose to look down.

built, the chances of finding one on the road were extremely slim. They did come with 3-litre engines, which was signficant for the 1975 model year.

Not only was the 3-litres capacity chosen for the new Porsche 930 or 911 Turbo for 1975, it was also the displacement of the new Carrera 3. Replacing the 911 S as the new middle-of-the-range 911, the Carrera 3 could still boast a decent turn of speed with 60 mph coming in 6 seconds and 100 mph in just 15.2, but the word Carrera hardly meant the same any more. Improved heaters, electrically operated and heated door mirrors, even optional cruise control were all incorporated into the Carrera specification before the name was finally dropped in mid-1977. The 911 SC took over the mantle.

We had to wait until 1984 for a new car with the Carrera name tag. Some still consider it a Carrera in name only. Yet there is no doubting the present car's abilities: 3.2-litres, 231 bhp and 209 lb ft of torque combine to throw you up the road at 152 mph if you do not have to worry about the speed limits. While advances in almost every other department set out to prove that the need to compromise comfort and practicality to enjoy the benefits of such exciting performance is a thing of the past.

Although the 935 racing version was very much in the early Carrera mould, the 930 road car was the flagship and as such offered the highest levels of luxury available from Porsche at the time. It is worth noting that even the 934 racer came with many of the road car comforts including electric windows as it had to make the relatively high Group 4 minimum weight.

Originally, the only reason we had a 911 Turbo road car was so the factory could homologate the racers for the new FIA Appendix J rules for the 1976 season. Porsche were testing turbocharged 911 RSRs at Le Mans as early as March 1974 in anticipation of the new rules, so the launch of the road car at the Paris Show in October of that year was a natural progression.

As stated previously, this was no hot rod. In standard form, the Turbo came with air conditioning, electric windows, leather upholstery, tinted glass, headlamp washers, rear window wiper and a price tag that left you in doubt as to intentions—almost twice the price of the standard 911. At that price, plus the fact that the launch came right on top of the oil crisis and general world recession, you could have forgiven Porsche for thinking that the planned 500 homologation production run would be all the Turbos they would ever sell. In the UK, total Porsche sales in 1975 went down to only 200 cars from a high of 600 the year

1987 Turbo SE. Top of the tree as far as readily available Porsches go.

Above
First used in 1952, the Porsche badge was a mixture of symbols. The antlers are part of the arms of the State of Wurttemburg, while the central shield with the black horse is from the arms of the city of Stuttgart. A horse because 'Stuttgart' came from the German for Stud Garden, as in horses. Easy really.

Right
1972 Carrera RS. Ducktail rear spoiler, little front air dam and enough graphics to make even sleeping Policemen sit up and take notice.

before. And only 50 Turbos were sold in the UK that year.

Still, somebody must have been buying them because a total of 1,300 Turbos were built in the first two years. And of course, the car is just as important part of the Porsche range today as it was then.

The first Turbos produced 260 bhp from 2994 cc; with a bore and stroke of 95 × 70.4 mm. And to cope with the extra torque (up to 253 lb ft compared with the Carrera's 188) they came with a bigger clutch and a new four-speed-only gearbox. In fact, it is only very recently that Porsche has given the Turbo five gears, in the same way that it took them many years to accept that the Targa or Cabriolet body could handle the power of the turbocharged engine.

Because of the nature of the turbo, the 0–60 mph time was no better than the Carrera, but once you got the car on the road, the difference became apparent, especially in the 60–100 mph range. There was power when you needed it, yet the car was perfectly docile when you did not. The Turbo may have looked like a racer, with its 8 inch rear wheels, giant flared arches and whale-tail rear spoiler, but its ease of driving and general lack of fuss was complimentary to the Porsche level of engineering skills and attention to driver comfort.

It is perhaps indicative of the excellence of that first Turbo package that the 930 has undergone only one major change since. In 1975 the bodyshell gained the Porsche six year warranty along with a 12 month unlimited mileage guarantee. In 1976 they added an electrically operated and heated door mirror and for 1977 the forged alloy five-spoke wheels with their wide low-profile Pirelli P7s were upped to 16 inches. Mechanical modifications were mainly aimed at smoothing the sudden rush of the turbo as the revs hit 3000 rpm, though 1977 also saw servo assistance for the brakes, albeit for the left hand drive models only.

For the 1983 Carrera 80 per cent of the engine was new.

Improvements of a major nature came in the 1978 model year as capacity grew to 3299 cc. An intercooler was squeezed beneath a modified rear spoiler and with no less than 300 bhp under the right foot, drivers were no doubt thankful that brakes were uprated too. An improved clutch design meant that the engine was actually moved back in the car for 1978, but if it made any difference to the car's manners they were certainly hard to detect. With its combination of acceleration figures of 0–60 mph in just 5.3 seconds and everyday practicality, the 911 Turbo had for many become the ultimate supercar. That it was improved yet again in 1983, when slight engine revisions pushed torque figures to even greater levels, was the icing on the cake.

As the 1989 model year Porsche 911 sales brochure proudly boasts, 'In June 1984 a standard production Porsche 911 Turbo won the title: "The Fastest Accelerating Production car in the World"; the first official event of its kind organised by the RAC Motor Sports Association. The final winning time, from a standing start to the one kilometre mark, was 23.985 seconds with a final speed of 135 mph. To date this achievement has not been bettered.'

While there are a whole number of production cars that may well be waiting for a chance to lay claim to that title, there can be few that could temper that awesome turn of speed with the practicality and everyday driveability of the 911 Turbo. And there are definitely none that can match its availability and continuous popularity.

As is typical of Porsche, as soon as one product is nearing perfection, there is another coming round the corner. And in the Turbo's case, that something else has been coming round the corner since 1983.

Inset
Looking good. But then at another £45,000 in advance of the price of a normal Turbo, it jolly well ought to.

Part of a dealer's test fleet, though not everybody gets a test that easily.

Visitors to the **Frankfurt Show** in 1983 were given the rare treat of an entirely new 911 derivative, though some might say that its only concession to the 911 concept is its roof line and engine configuration. The *Gruppe B* design study that appeared that year set the course for Porsche road car development that is now a reality.

Designed with **Group B** rally competition in mind, the 959, as it became known, would have to compete with a number of other low production homologation specials that formed the winning nucleus in the top class of international competition. In very basic terms, it needed the speed of a Formula 1 racing car, the body of a production saloon and the suspension and handling characteristics to

The first Bosch Digital Motor Electronics system, a black box under the driver's seat, was used in the 1983 Carrera.

enable it to use the performance to the full. Best of all, Porsche had to produce 200 road going production versions to homologate it for competition use.

Although, as we now know, the full international rally car was never allowed to compete, thanks to a change in the rules which effectively banned that sort of car for international rallying, it is no less interesting to chart its progress from design study to fruition.

That Porsche had the capability and the know-how to produce the power required was

Capacity was stretched to 3164 cc in 1983.

never in question. The production 959's 450 bhp from 2850 cc of twin-turbocharged flat six is hardly anything to write home about in Porsche terms. It was the four-wheel drive system that needed the development and the engineering investment.

Early plans called for a six-speed gearbox— five normal plus a **G** (Gelände) gear that was not unlike an 'extra low' for off-road use in bad conditions—with a variable torque split system that was electronically driver-controlled to match the terrain. The system that first emerged, however, was much simpler.

Jacky Ickx persuaded Porsche to enter two cars in the 1984 Paris Dakar rally and it was these cars that were the first four-wheel drive guinea pigs. That early simplified system used a mechanical centre differential lock, the normal five-speed transmission and a 3-litre Carrera engine, detuned to 225 bhp to cope with the low-grade African fuel. The fact that both cars finished a 12,000 km race that claimed most of its starters was obviously encouraging.

A year later Porsche were back in the desert with cars that were a lot nearer to the 959 concept. Six-speed transmissions, wild swoopy bodywork, extensive use of the latest composite materials including Kevlar, but still only 230 bhp Carrera engines and a mechanical torque split. None of the Porsche entrants lasted the course that year, but it was through no fault of the transmission.

The brakes were bigger with a bigger servo.

The final production 959 is for the moment at least, the ultimate Porsche road car. So awesome is its specification, not to mention the prices it seems to be fetching, that it has stolen the limelight almost completely from its humbler and readily available four-wheel drive brother, the 911 Carrera 4.

In many respects, the 959 takes production car technology into a new era. Like the 930 Turbo before it, this is no stripped out, go-faster hot rod; it's a well mannered, practical, all-weather motor car as any of its 250 very lucky (not to mention very rich) owners will confirm. Design features include water-cooled heads, 24 valves and a twin-turbo system that uses just the one turbo up to 4300 rpm, then blasts you with the other one right up to the 369 bhp maximum at 5500 rpm. It has a six-speed transmission and a very sophisticated four-wheel drive system with wheel sensors that detect slip and automatically transfer drive to the front wheels via a hydraulically controlled multi-plate clutch until a 50–50 front and rear maximum is obtained. Include the endless other bits of technology-in-action, like the anti-lock brakes, the speed controlled

Maximum speed was up to 152 mph by 1983.

More fun on the Paris–Dakar. Rothmans team rush about trying to get to Dakar in the shortest possible time, while bemused spectators wonder why.
Rothmans

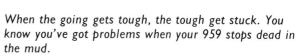

When the going gets tough, the tough get stuck. You know you've got problems when your 959 stops dead in the mud.
Rothmans

automatic self-levelling, and it's easy to see why the 959 is so important to Porsche as a testbed for many features that will be taken for granted as typical of a production Porsche in the future.

This is true to some extent already, of course. The Carrera 4, or the 964 as it was known in its prototype stages, may look much like the previous Carrera except for deformable bumpers and automatically adjusting speed-sensitive rear spoiler, but closer examination reveals just how different the car really is.

For a start there is an entirely new floorpan. Gone finally are the torsion bars front and rear. These are replaced by coil springs. And there is power-assisted steering, ABS brakes and something else new to Porsche, negative scrub radius for the front suspension geometry which generates automatic steering correction in the event of uneven tyre grip under braking.

Engine capacity has gone up once again to 3.6-litres with twin ignition systems and 250 bhp. Though what is of more interest is that

That's the thing about the Paris–Dakar . . .
Rothmans

Above
Sometimes it's desert . . .
Rothmans

Left
Other times it's mountain. Either way, roads are not exactly thick on the ground. Mud is an unexpected hazard in the Sahara.
Rothmans

the **US**-spec reduced emissions version delivers the same power output, giving the Americans 33 bhp more than the 1988 Carrera. Apparently, this is part of a new Porsche policy to offer the same performance both sides of the Atlantic.

Looking to the future, plans are already well advanced for a two-wheel drive version of the Carrera 4 and in 1991 we will see the replacement for the 911 Turbo. As we go to press, the Porsche 965 (though it may well have a different name by the time it goes public), will look very much like the 959, only slightly smoother in profile with more rounded safety bumpers fore and aft. It will keep that flat nose, and the distinctive rear spoiler treatment, but beneath it will hide yet another development of the Porsche flat-six—a version of the new Carrera 4 motor, probably with twin-plug heads

Fun at Le Mans. Racing version of the 959, the 961, driven by Rene Metge and Claude Ballot-Lena, it finished seventh in 1986.
Tony Thacker

Above
One of Porsche's 959 cutaway show cars. Technology in action. Twin water-cooled turbochargers with air-to-air intercoolers, 450 bhp and 500 nm of torque.

Right
Just in case you get one in the rear view mirror, this is what a 959 will look like. Don't worry though, it won't stay there for very long.

and possibly with twin turbos too. **Naturally the 965 will combine ABS brakes with the new six-speed transmission and four-wheel drive, though this will probably be a simplified version of the 959's costly electronically controlled variable torque split system.**

So while it true to say that the evolution of the 911 concept has progressed to a point where future models will bear only the slightest resemblence to those of the past, it would be very shortsighted indeed to view the present models in isolation. The 901 prototype is as much a part of the 959's heritage as the 959 will be of whatever Porsche offer us in another 25 years time.

And that Porsche 911-based cars will be as popular then as they are now, there is no doubt.

Right
*Whichever way you look at it, a 959
is a beautiful shape.*

Above
*There's no mistaking that rear
spoiler either.*

Left
1972 Carrera. Looking good from any angle, the 1972 Carrera will always be one of the most collectable and indeed copied Porsches. Though it must be said that if you haven't got one already, you'll have to save up for a very long time.
Autocar

Right
911 Turbo at Le Mans in 1985.
Malcolm Bryant

Above
Another Turbo. In its most modern guise, the turbo engine throws out 300 bhp and 430 nm of torque, enough to fling you up the road at 160 mph.
Autocar

Left
Until quite recently, 911 Turbo rear arches were grafted on seperately at the factory. New Turbos have one-piece rear wings.

Bill Taylor's Carrera RS, track tested by Motor Magazine
Motor

Previous page
3.3 Turbo with snazzy plaid trim.
Chris Harvey

Above
1976 Carrera 3 with distinctive black graphics.
Chris Harvey

Right
3.0 RSR. Basically a 1974 RS Carrera modified for racing with wider wings and wheels—10.5 inches front and 14 inches at the rear.
Chris Harvey

The next wave. 1989 Carrera 4. The new rear spoiler is elevated in proportion to acceleration. As speed declines it sinks more slowly just in case the driver goes back on throttle.

959 in all its silver glory. It may lean but it will not let go. Just as handy in the wet too.

Above
Not exactly the thing for bumping up high kerbs, this body kit will set you back around £5000.

Left
Dage Sport Turbo. Another flat nose styling package for the lucky few. Comes with 400 bhp, 0–60 mph in 4.4 seconds and 0–100 mph in 10.1.

Following page
911SE at the London Motor Show in 1985.

AFN Ltd. Isleworth

Charles Follett Ltd. Mayfair

Motortune Ltd. Chelsea

Charles Follett (Barbican) Ltd

Evolution

As long as there have been Porsches, there have been racing Porsches. And without doubt, it was the 911 that put Porsche on the map as far as racing success was concerned. Barely four months after the first example had rolled off the production line in 1964, a 911 was entered in the Monte Carlo rally. It not only cleaned up in the GT class but took a very creditable fifth place overall, behind another Porsche, the 'proper' racing mid-engined 904 in second place only to Timo Makinen's flying Mini Cooper. From then on the name Porsche would appear in the winner's circle at almost every event they entered, whether it was in rally competition or on the track.

Proving right from the start that they were not going to take competition lightly, that first 911 competition car was piloted by two Porsche factory engineers, Herbert Linge and Peter Falk. The engine was lightly tuned for an extra 30 bhp and there were subtle but important changes to both suspension and braking. Their class win set the standard for Porsche rally success that was to last until the end of the decade.

To prove that the Monte was no fluke, German driver Gunther Klass won the European GT Rally Championship the following year, taking the German Rally outright, while other drivers triumphed with an outright win in the Austrian Alpine Rally.

By 1966, of course, the teams had the 911 S and with more power to play with. The result was almost a forgone conclusion. The factory-backed team of Vic Elford and David Stone took the European GT Rally Championship for a second year running, while private teams did well thanks to the Porsche Stage 1 and 2 rally tuning kits offered for the 911 S, raising power to 170 and 175 bhp respectively.

Side by side at Zandvoort. Chris Millard's 3-litre Turbo (left) dices with the ubiquitous Bill Taylor.
Chris Harvey

The 1988 Classic Marathon. Paul Brace gives lessons in Porsche cornering in Chris Harvey's 911ST.
Chris Harvey

Inset
One of only 22, double rare 911Rs, caught at Brands Hatch in 1979. Car is now fully restored.
Chris Harvey

It's worth noting too, that by now the 911 was making its presence felt in other forms of competition. Private Porsche teams were winning their classes in both hillclimbing and endurance racing. GT class wins at Spa, Daytona, Sebring, the Nürburgring and the Targa Florio were all clocked up for the first time in the 1967 season, and it would be many years before anyone else even got a look in.

The 911 R (R for *Rennsport* or racing) appeared in 1967 and was substantially lightened with many fibreglass and plastic parts. The spartan interior featured two deep bucket seats and very little else and the engine pushed out no less than 210 bhp. Sadly only 22 of these machines were built as Porsche decided against homologation so for all its power, the 911 R never really had a chance to prove what it could do, though it did manage to establish five world records on the Monza banked circuits in 1967. Something else it proved was the strength and reliability of the new Porsche Sportomatic four-speed semi-automatic transmission fitted to the winning 911 R in the *Marathon de la Route*, a 24-hour high speed trial at the Nürburgring.

For the rest of the 1960 s, rally competition was Porsche all the way. In 1968 Pauli Toivonen clinched the World Rally Championship in his 180 bhp 911 T, his second place on the Monte Carlo only due to being pipped by another 911

T in the very capable hands of Vic Elford and David Stone. In 1969 it was Bjorn Waldegaard's turn to win the Monte, while Toivonen took the testing Acropolis Rally, and in 1970 Porsche made it the hat-trick, with Bjorn Waldegaard and Lars Helmer taking the Monte once again, just in front of the Gerard Larrousse-Maurice Gelin team in another 911 ST. Needless to say, Porsche took yet another World Rally Championship that year.

The 911 ST was another of the limited edition race-only 911 based cars. By 1969, the 911 S had the benefit of 2.2-litres and longer wheelbase. The 911 ST added to this advantage with

Closer inspection reveals more 911 design features than you would think in a 356 C.
Chris Harvey

Right
One of only 109, and 50 of those were built to the higher RSR spec. 3.0 RS, hillclimbing at Prescott.
Chris Harvey

thinner steel in many parts, extensive use of fibreglass and severe lightening throughout. With 240 bhp from the further bored 2.2-litre engine (up to 2247 cc), it was no wonder the competition melted into the distance.

The 1970 s were not great years for Porsche rally cars. With more of the valuable Weissach development time going to the turbocharged cars and the little Alpine Renaults set to dominate the European rally circuit, most of Porsche's efforts were reserved for the tough African Safari rally. Despite ever more powerful engines and visits to Africa in 1971, 1972, 1974 and 1978, a victory eluded every Porsche team that entered, more often than not due to suspension failure. True, they scored a second overall in 1972, another in 1974 and yet another in 1978, but at Porsche, second is not enough.

Porsche managed the odd second in Europe too; they even won the Monte Carlo in 1978, but the heady days of the late 1960 s were never matched. And besides, when you are winning everything in sight on the track anyway, the lack of success in rally circles was hardly the end of the world.

Already mentioned were the beginnings of Porsche 911 success at the racetrack with GT wins at Sebring, Spa and others as early as 1967. But by the late 1960s Porsche 911s were homologated for many different classes of racing, and winning convincingly in all of them. The 911 and 911 L fitted nicely into Group 2 Touring, the 911 T and 911 S were homologated for Group 3 GT and if you were lucky enough to own one of the few 911 Rs, you could compete with the proper Porsche race cars in the prototype classes.

In 1968 a Porsche 911 took the chequered flag at the *Marathon de la Route* with GT victories at the Nürburgring, Watkins Glen, Le Mans, Monza, Sebring and the Targa Florio. And in 1969, they did exactly the same thing at nearly all the same places, which is probably why the rules were changed for 1970, banning Porsche completely from saloon car racing. Still, they did take the World Rally Championship that year, plus the World Championship in endurance racing with the 917 and 908/3 models.

911 racing. Bill Taylor's Carrera RS at Snetterton.
Chris Harvey

620 horses worth of Porsche six-pot.
Hardly a D-I-Y service job.

Left
Another view of the 959. Front axle
with four-wheel drive and more than
its fair share of high technology.

Right
935. The only view most of the
competition ever got. 1974 Carrera
RSR in Martini trim.
Martini

It's unlikely Porsche was much concerned by the saloon car rule adjustments.

If the 1960s counted as golden years for Porsche rally success, then track success in the 1970s would definitely make them platinum by comparison with a string of international victories that was as impressive as the cars that earned them. Monza, Spa, Le Mans, Targa Florio, Nürburgring, they all fell to Porsche with alarming regularity in the early part of the decade. And that was just the 911, though it has to be said that as the era passed, the racing 911s moved further and further away from their road-going counterparts.

At first it was the 911 ST, taking the GT class at almost every World Championship endurance race it entered. And in 1972 it was the turn of a 2.5-litre version of the newly

911s on the streets of Birmingham. Mike Burtt's Carrera Club Sport leads Bill Taylor's RS.
Chris Harvey

increased 2.4-litre road car with wide wheels under flared arches, a small front spoiler and no less than 270 bhp to draw on. It was hardly surprising it took the European Grand Touring Car Championship, the Porsche Cup and the IMSA Camel GT Championship that year.

The Carrera had its year in 1973. Introduced at the Paris Salon a year earlier, the Carrera RS was Porsche's answer to increasing competition in the GT classes. The original intention was to build 500 of them to homologate it into Group 4, though the RS and its racing counterpart, the awesome RSR proved so successful that they had produced twice that many by April 1973.

Silverstone in 1977. A 935/77. The first year for twin turbochargers.
Chris Harvey

The production Carrera RS were available in three different versions. The M471 RS Sport, which has become known as the 'lightweight', came with little in the way of interior comfort save a pair of bucket seats, rubber floor mats and a passenger sunvisor. The M472 RS Touring was the most common variant with slightly more luxury. And the M491 RS Rennsport came with a 2.8-litre unit. Only 49 were built. One of the most covetted 911s by modern enthusiasts, the RSR, boasted more than 300 bhp that first year, so it was hardly surprising that it took the Daytona 24 Hours even before it was properly homologated for Group 4. It was all the more notable as the first outright victory in the

World Championship by a production-based Porsche. They took the last Targa Florio and almost every round of the European GT Championship that year too.

By 1974 things were getting serious. The Carrera RS was bored out to 3.0-litres, which translated to 230 bhp, while the RSR went up to 330 bhp. As an evolution of the 1973 car, Porsche were only required to build 100 1974 versions for homologation purposes, though a total of 109 managed to escape from the factory that year. Some 15 of these went to the American IROC series, 50 made RSR spec and the rest became the extremely desirable road-going versions. And while they all sported flared arches, giant US-spec front bumpers and whale-tail rear spoilers, the RSR versions looked even wilder thanks to vented arches

Lightweight tube frame plus high performance 911 motor makes a dangerous combination. This is the Canepa Porsche, driven by Paul Newman at Devil's Playground.

front and rear and immense centre lock wheels (10.5 inch front and 14 inch rear).

Success was inevitable and in 1974 and 1975. The RSR, by now competing in Group 5, took both European GT and American IMSA Championships.

However, as anyone who witnessed the unveiling of the new Porsche 930 (the 911 turbo) prototype at the 1973 Frankfurt Show would have realised, change was in the air. And with six months still to go before the introduction of the road car, Porsche were testing turbo-charged racing cars at Le Mans in preparation for the coming silhouette formula for Group 5 cars.

With at least 450 bhp on tap depending on how high you pushed the boost, the RSR Turbo heralded a whole new era in Porsche engine design. Running as a 3.0-litre prototype, though reduced to 2.2-litres to accomodate the FIA's 1.4 capacity multiplier for turbocharged cars, it boasted such luxurious racing items as titanium conrods and a magnesium crankcase to complement the single KKK turbocharger running at between 1.3 and 1.5 atmospheres of boost. Underneath, the rear suspension was now hung on its own spaceframe with alloy trailing arms and titanium axles, while springing was coils all round. With its deeper front spoiler, giant rear wing and striking Martini colours, the turbo obviously meant business. And while it may not have been the most successful racing car in 911 history, it did its job. That is, to pave the way for the new 1976 cars. The real turbo racers.

With the whole of the 1975 season off to develop something new, it was hardly surprising that the results were something special. To homologate the 1976 race cars, Porsche had introduced the 930 in 1975 with plans for only the minimum requirement of 400 cars. That they are still producing it some thirteen years later speaks volumes about the integrity of its design. And that the racing

versions were not so far removed from those production models says even more. There were two racing versions of the 930: The 934, sold to private customers for Group 4 racing and the 935, which the factory team campaigned in Group 5.

For DM 108,000, a customer could take delivery of his very own Porsche 934, complete with all the racing necessities like roll cage and racing seat, but also most of the usual 930 comforts. Even the electric windows were left in to make up the 1120 kg weight break. It's a pity only 31 people took up the offer, because for all its weight, the car was spectacularly quick. Especially by the end of the season when teams were getting up to 580 bhp. And that was with standard turbo crankcase, crank, con-rods and heads. It is no wonder a 934 won the European GT Championship that year in the hands of Toine Hezemans. The 934 was banned from IMSA racing for 1976 and only competed in 1977 because Porsche built a special run of 10 IMSA-legal cars using many of the mechanical parts from the 935. With wider wheels, better fuel injection and much more power they were apparently much better cars to drive.

In 1976 form, the 935 ran slightly less capacity than the 934 so it could just scrape under the 4-litre mark once the 1.4 multiplier had done its worst. Though with nearly 600 bhp pulling only 970 kg, it was hardly going to be the slower of the two. Needless to say, it won the 1976 World Championship of Makes. In fact, by the end of its career, the 935 had become the most successful competition car ever, taking 42 World Championship and 70 IMSA wins.

By 1977 many of the previous year's private 934 customers had rebuilt their cars to 935 spec. Porsche helped another 13 lucky people out by supplying them with cars to race in Group 5 that year too, though as replicas of the 1976 model they were not quite as lucky as the people who got the three 1977 spec factory cars. 935s took first and second place at every single

Inset
A decade ago the name Martini became almost synonymous with Porsche racing success, giving both companies not only something to celebrate but something to celebrate with.
Martini

The Baby. The 935/2.0, a 370 bhp, turbocharged 1.4-litre special. Didn't do much first time out but on the second at Hockenheim, Ickx managed to lap most of the field for such a convincing win that the car was retired for good.
Martini

round of the championship in 1977, despite rule changes aimed at giving the competition a bit of a chance, though with 630 bhp from the new twin-turbo motor, a bit of a chance is all the competition did have. The twin turbos were not so much for the extra power, of course (though it obviously helped), but for the improved throttle response. Two smaller units were quicker to get spinning than a single counterpart.

The rule about defining the body silhouette as the bit between the front and rear bulkhead is what led to the famous flat-nosed 935, which finally made its way onto a Porsche 911 production car some ten years later. They also gained a false plexiglass rear window to improve the cars aerodynamics. After all, the rules may have stated that you had to retain the stock rear window but where did they say you could not have two?

By 1978, it was left up to private teams to wave the Porsche flag in the World Championship of Makes, as the factory team concentrated on Le Mans. The car they designed to do it with was the famous 935/78-Moby Dick.

Moby Dick took full advantage of the

silhouette rules to achieve a body that was as aerodynamic as the 911 roof line would allow. With maximum speed on the Mulsanne straight so crucial to Le Mans racers, Porsche even compromised downforce and cornering ability to this one aim. Built entirely around an aluminium tube frame, the body was lowered and the floor section was raised to regain the ground clearance. The engine, a twin-turbo unit with 3213 cc to get it just below the 4.5-litres once the FIA multiplied it up, developed a phenominal 750 bhp at 8200 rpm, partly due to the new water-cooled heads with twin over-head cams and four valves per cylinder. It certainly worked too. Moby Dick was nine seconds a lap faster round Le Mans than the 935/77 had been. It achieved 222 mph on the Mulsanne straight.

Yet for all its technology and all its speed, unreliability on the day meant that eighth place was all Porsche could manage in 1978. The factory team did not score any better in 1979. This spelt the end of factory involvement in the 935. Though it has to be pointed out that over half of the 23 finishers that year were Porsches and that nine of those were 935s. Erwin Kremer's own development of the 935, the K3, took the overall win in front of three other Porsches.

With the factory money going to the bigger, faster 956 and 962 endurance racers, it was the private teams that contributed most to 935 racing history. Porsche continued producing 935s for privateers up to 1979, of course, with improvements like detachable rear wings in 1978 and some of Moby Dick's better features in 1979, but the numbers were not great (15 cars in 1978) so most of the new 935s were built from scratch by independent companies like Kremer. Any racer rich enough to afford the DM 350,000 could have a Kremer K3 replica in 1980, or you could have bought one of their conversion kits if you fancied doing it yourself.

Many of these teams did very well too, taking

935/78. The longest of them all, Moby Dick. 3213 cc, 1030 kg and a whopping 750 bhp.

The car that launched a thousand flat noses. New silhouette rules meant that the 935 finally debuted with this streamlined front end. Martini

the World Championship of Makes in 1978 and 1979. The only reason they lost in 1980 and 1981 was because Lancia exploited a loophole in the rulebook. As the only entrant in the under 2-litre class they managed a perfect points score and took the overall Championship.

In 1982 the FIA changed the rules again. Groups 3, 4 and 5 became A, B and C and the 935 was about to make way for something even better. It had certainly had a good enough run for its money though, as the results confirm. World Championship of Makes four years running, no less than 70 IMSA victories, that famous Le Mans win in 1979 and some would say most impressive of all, the Daytona 24 Hours seven years on the trot up to 1983. And then it was only beaten by a March 83G with a 935 engine.

Porsche 911 based race cars had come the whole distance from that first Monte Carlo rally car in 1965 to become one of the most successful race cars of all time. The final versions may not have been much like the first, in fact they probably shared not one common part. But that is not the point. The Porsche 911 story is one of constant evolution, constant development and constant improvement. And more than anything, it was the race programme that dictated the way the road cars developed in the following years. That is why racing is so important to Porsche and that is why the Porsche enthusiast looks forward to each and every new racing machine. Because he or she knows that every racing Porsche is testing new ideas and new technology that will form an important part of the road car he or she be driving in years to come.

935/78 Moby Dick. Built solely for Le Mans, the 1978 bodywork traded grip in the corners for high-speed aerodynamics down the Mulsanne Straight.
Chris Harvey

935 Kremer K4, built by the Kremer brothers after they had gained access to the factory's Moby Dick plans, though they did alter the bodywork for more down force in the bends.
Chris Harvey

Above
Brands Hatch in 1984. An American 935.
Malcolm Bryant

Right
The 1972 Targa Florio, one of Porsche's many GT class wins that year.

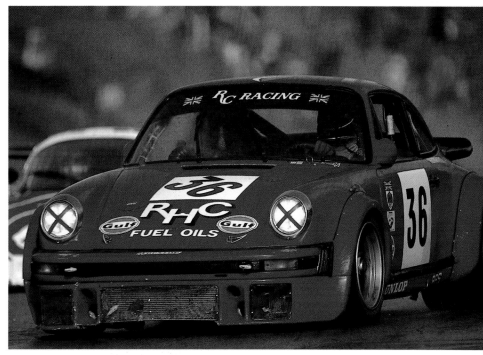

Above
934 shows them how to do it; 330 bhp to start with, though later versions managed well over 500.

Left
More 935 styling. This time at Brands Hatch in 1982. A Danish entry from J. Poulsen and Pete Hansen.
Malcolm Byrant

Below
Swapping motors on a Carrera RSR must be fun at the best of times, but in the pits at the Nürburgring, it takes on another dimension altogether.
Chris Harvey

The East African Safari car for 1974.
Basically a modified 1973 Carrera
RS, but reinforced and raised up a
bit to clear stray East African
boulders.
Chris Harvey

East African Safari car. Beautiful
paintwork, but the East African was
one of Porsche's biggest
disappointments.
Rothmans

Left
John Greasley's 935 K3 at Silverstone. Built from Kevlar, the K3 had raised edges on both front and rear wings to keep the air on them, and so improving the downforce.
Chris Harvey

Above
Keith Russell's Carrera RS at Brands in 1988.
Chris Harvey

Above
John Bell's 934 at Oulton Park in 1984.
Chris Harvey

Right
Turbocharged 3.0 RSR at Brands back in 1976, though they debuted in 1974.
Chris Harvey

Porsche managed first and second on the Paris–Dakar in 1986—on the third time of trying.
Rothmans

*Just because it's dark, it doesn't
mean you have to stop racing.*
Rothmans

Rothmans